THIS BOOK BELONGS TO:

When Dad Disappeared

Author:

Monica Garrett

Illustrator :

Palwasha Sajid

When Dad Disappeared

Author: Monica Garrett

Illustrator: Palwasha Sajid

Interior Layout Designer: Abdul_moeez

Email: GarrettsScriptedCorner@gmail.com

Dedication

To our son Maceo, who always motivate me to do and be more. Although your Dad's life was short, I will always ensure to keep his memories alive for as long as I shall live. Mom and Dad always love you!

It's early morning, and the sun is shining brightly. Mom is at work and I just gotten out of bed. I started playing with my toys in the kitchen with Dad while he cooks breakfast.

He cooks my favorite scrambled eggs. Now it's time for us to eat. We have scrambled eggs, toast, fruit and milk to drink.

Dad is doing homework while I watch cartoons. I like watching cartoons while eating my food. "My eggs are delicious, Dad," I said. "Thank you very much, son," said Dad. After I finished eating, Dad gave me another one of my favorites, the famous applesauce!

I see my Dad's cell phone and his keys. I grabbed them and started playing with them. I opened a cartoon video to watch on his phone. I also started pressing buttons on his keys. The buttons cause his truck's horn to beep, beep, beep. Dad is finishing his homework before we go outside.

We went outside to enjoy the nice weather and hot sun. As I'm riding on my 3-wheeler down the street, my Dad walks alongside me to protect me and as part of his daily exercise. "I can't wait for Mom to come home," I said to Dad. "Yes, son, I can't wait either", said Dad. We went around the block, and on our way home, we saw Mom turning in the driveway of our home. "Yesssss Mom is home," I said to Dad! I peddled fast to get home.

Mom waits for us in the driveway to make it home. I hurried off my 3-wheel bike, ran, and gave Mom a big hug and a kiss. Hi Mom, I said! Dad and Mom hug and kiss as well, happy to see each other. "Welcome home, babe," Dad says to Mom.

We all walked inside the house. Dad has to leave to get his hair cut, and then we're going bowling when he returns. I enjoy bowling. We go bowling every time. Dad takes out his phone and keys. Before leaving, he gives Mom and me a hug and kiss and says, "I love you." "We love you too", Mom and I said to Dad. Dad leaves home, and mom cooks dinner.

The weather was still nice outside. After eating dinner, Mom and I went back outside so I could ride my power wheel car. I like driving my power wheel because it goes fast. I also like to press the buttons on it because it makes the siren go off and the lights flash. I'm driving down the street with my Mom walking behind me. We were outside for a while. We went around two blocks in the neighborhood.

On our way home, we saw two police cars driving down the street, and then they stopped in front of our home. The police officers walked up to my Mom and started talking to her. Then I saw my Mom crying. I was confused and did not know what was wrong with my Mom and why she was crying or what was going on. It started getting dark outside and Dad never came back home.

A few days later, I saw my Dad's phone and keys but did not see him. I wanted to play with them, but my Mom put them away with tears in her eyes. I never knew what happened to my Dad, but as I grew older, the more questions I asked my Mom. I was too young to understand, but my Mom always explained what happened to me so that I would remember as I grew older. Mom would always tell me that my Dad is not here with us, but he could see us. I could talk to him, speak about him, look at photos and watch videos of him at any time. My Mom and I always looked through our family photos to remember Dad. Mom says "You grow up and be a great kid son. Dad is always watching over us every step of the way."

Write a letter to the person (or something) that is very special to you that has passed away or currently still alive and let them know how you feel about them. When complete, write your name and today's date.

Draw a picture of you and the person (or something) that has passed or currently still alive and is very special to you having fun together. When complete, write today's date.